W9-CFQ-565

SYMBOLS OF AMERICA

THE BALD EAGLE

BY MARIA NELSON

Gareth Stevens
PUBLISHING

Please visit our website, www.garethstevens.com. For a free color catalog of all our high-quality books, call toll free 1-800-542-2595 or fax 1-877-542-2596.

Library of Congress Cataloging-in-Publication Data

Nelson, Maria.
The bald eagle / by Maria Nelson.
p. cm. — (Symbols of America)
Includes index.
ISBN 978-1-4824-1867-5 (pbk.)
ISBN 978-1-4824-1865-1 (6-pack)
ISBN 978-1-4824-1866-8 (library binding)
1. United States — Seal — Juvenile literature. 2. Bald eagle — United States — Juvenile literature. 3. Emblems, National — United States — Juvenile literature. I. Nelson, Maria. II. Title.
CD5610.N45 2015
929.90973—d23

Published in 2015 by
Gareth Stevens Publishing
111 East 14th Street, Suite 349
New York, NY 10003

Copyright © 2015 Gareth Stevens Publishing

Designer: Sarah Liddell
Editor: Kristen Rajczak

Photo credits: Cover, p. 1 Rihardzz/Shutterstock.com; p. 5 Teri Virbickis/Shutterstock.com; p. 7 Mayskyphoto/Shutterstock.com; p. 9 Jim Barber/Shutterstock.com; p. 11 Deanne/Shutterstock.com; p. 13 Georgios Kollidas/Shutterstock.com; p. 15 Steve Collender/Shutterstock.com; p. 17 spirit of america/Shutterstock.com; p. 19 lendy16/Shutterstock.com; p. 21 Sergey Uryadnikov/Shutterstock.com.

Printed in the United States of America

CPSIA compliance information: Batch #CW15GS: For further information contact Gareth Stevens, New York, New York at 1-800-542-2595.

CONTENTS

Boldface words appear in the glossary.

Important Bird

The American bald eagle is the national bird of the United States. It's a strong and beautiful bird. Since early in our country's history, this proud eagle has been the national **emblem**.

The American bald eagle is easy to spot. It's mostly brown with a white head and tail. It's not bald, though! It has feathers on its head. An old meaning of "bald" is "marked with white."

The Great Seal

In 1782, the **likeness** of an American bald eagle was used for the Great Seal of the United States. It has a **shield** on its chest. It holds an olive branch in its right **talons** and 13 arrows in its left talons.

Choosing the Emblem

The Founding Fathers spent years fighting about what the official US emblem should be. It wasn't until 1789 that the American bald eagle was chosen. It was also named the national bird then.

Ben Franklin wrote in a letter that he thought the bald eagle on the national emblem looked like a turkey. Then, he wrote that he thought the turkey was a more "respectable" bird than the eagle!

13

Flying Free

The American bald eagle was chosen as the emblem because it's native to the United States. It was also thought to be a great **symbol** for the United States' strength and freedom.

Often Seen

Since it's on the Great Seal, the American bald eagle is seen on many papers and government buildings throughout the country. The US president's flag has a picture of the American bald eagle on it, too.

E PLURIBUS UNUM

17

The American bald eagle first appeared on a coin in Massachusetts in 1776. It's been on half dollars, silver dollars, and quarters that are still used today. The American bald eagle is also on the $1 bill!

Protected

The American bald eagle population was very low during the 1900s. In 1940, a law made it illegal to hunt or harm bald eagles. It's important to **protect** one of the greatest national symbols!

TIMELINE OF THE NATIONAL EMBLEM

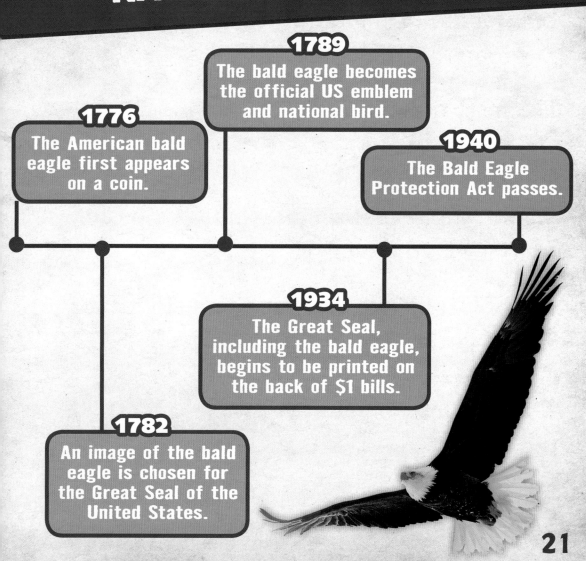

1789
The bald eagle becomes the official US emblem and national bird.

1776
The American bald eagle first appears on a coin.

1940
The Bald Eagle Protection Act passes.

1934
The Great Seal, including the bald eagle, begins to be printed on the back of $1 bills.

1782
An image of the bald eagle is chosen for the Great Seal of the United States.

GLOSSARY

emblem: a sign that represents a person or group

likeness: a picture

protect: to keep safe

shield: a piece of armor worn on the arm used to protect oneself

symbol: a picture or shape that stands for something else

talon: one of a bird's sharp claws

FOR MORE INFORMATION

BOOKS

Goldsworthy, Kaite. *Bald Eagle*. New York, NY: AV2 by Weigl, 2013.

Marcovitz, Hal. *Bald Eagle: The Story of Our National Bird*. Broomall, PA: Mason Crest, 2014.

WEBSITES

National Bird—American Bald Eagle
statesymbolsusa.org/National_Symbols/Bird_bald_eagle.html
Read about the history of the bald eagle as a symbol, and learn about the bird, too.

Symbols of US Government: The Bald Eagle
bensguide.gpo.gov/3-5/symbols/eagle.html
This website gives information and links to more sites about the bald eagle as a US symbol.

INDEX